£6·95

MARIO BELLINI

DESIGNER

MARIO BELLINI

DESIGNER

Cara McCarty

The Museum of Modern Art, New York

PUBLISHED ON THE OCCASION OF THE EXHIBITION
"MARIO BELLINI: DESIGNER," JUNE 24-SEPTEMBER 15, 1987,
DIRECTED BY CARA McCARTY, ASSISTANT CURATOR,
DEPARTMENT OF ARCHITECTURE AND DESIGN,
THE MUSEUM OF MODERN ART

THIS EXHIBITION HAS BEEN MADE POSSIBLE BY GENEROUS
SUPPORT FROM OLIVETTI; CASSINA, S.P.A.; BRIONVEGA; LANCIA;
VITRA SEATING, INC.; AND ERCO LEUCHTEN. ADDITIONAL FUNDING
HAS BEEN PROVIDED BY THE NATIONAL ENDOWMENT FOR THE ARTS.

EDITED BY SUSAN WEILEY
DESIGNED BY STEVEN SCHOENFELDER
PRODUCTION BY DANIEL FRANK
TYPE SET BY CONCEPT TYPOGRAPHIC SERVICES, NEW YORK
COLOR SEPARATIONS BY SPECTRA II SEPARATIONS, NEW YORK
PRINTED BY EASTERN PRESS, INC., NEW HAVEN, CONNECTICUT
BOUND BY MUELLER TRADE BINDERY, MIDDLETOWN, CONNECTICUT

THE MUSEUM OF MODERN ART
11 WEST 53 STREET, NEW YORK, NEW YORK 10019
PRINTED IN THE UNITED STATES OF AMERICA
COVER: DETAIL OF P101 ELECTRONIC DESKTOP COMPUTER. 1965.
FRONTISPIECE: MARIO BELLINI

CONTENTS

On behalf of The Museum of Modern Art, I wish to thank Mario Bellini for his cordial personal cooperation and for making this project a very gratifying experience.

In the Studio Bellini, special recognition is due to Agata Torricella for her unfailing competence as a liaison, coordinating all matters pertaining to the documentation and organization of Bellini's work for the exhibition as well as assisting with the installation design. In the same office, Dario Bellini, Adriana Sinigaglia, and Elena Bellini have helped greatly.

I am likewise grateful to Franco Perotti and Alessandro Chiarato, members of Olivetti's design studio, who have been especially helpful and patient in fulfilling my numerous requests regarding Olivetti products.

I would like to express sincerest appreciation to the exhibition sponsors: Ennio Brion of Brionvega; Rodrigo Rodriquez of Cassina; Klaus-Juergen Maack of Erco Leuchten; Oddone Camerana of Fiat Auto; Paolo Viti of Olivetti; and Rolf Fehlbaum of Vitra International. They have not only generously contributed to the exhibition, but have graciously prepared and lent their products. Paolo Viti deserves particular admiration and thanks for arranging the consortium of sponsors for the exhibition.

In addition, I am grateful to Piero Busnelli of B & B Italia for familiarizing me with industrial processes and materials and for his generous cooperation in lending to the exhibition. I appreciate the efforts of Arturo C. Quintavalle, Director of the Centro Studi e Archivio della Comunicazione, University of Parma, for placing Bellini's archives at my disposal.

For the preparation of this catalog, I am indebted to Susan Weiley whose enthusiasm and editorial skills brought clarity to the text. I also thank Daniel Frank who oversaw the production and Harriet Bee for her initial reading of the manuscript. Steven Schoenfelder's elegant book design is a significant contribution to this publication.

As always, it has been a pleasure to work with fellow staff members in the Department of Architecture and Design, without whose efforts this exhibition would not have been realized. I wish to thank Stuart Wrede for his reading of the manuscript and helpful suggestions concerning the exhibition. This text has benefited from my conversations with Robert Coates, whose encouragement, good humor, and talented assistance with the exhibition design have been indispensable. Christopher Mount was especially helpful with organizing the checklist and the photographic material, and Florence Zaragoza typed the manuscript.

No individual deserves my deepest personal thanks more than Arthur Drexler, former Director of the Department of Architecture and Design. It was Arthur who gave me the opportunity and encouragement to do this publication and accompanying exhibition. Although he did not live long enough to see either to fruition, the lessons and standards he taught me have been a guiding force in the preparation of both projects. It was a privilege to work for Arthur. He taught me how to see.

C. M.

INTRODUCTION

Mario Bellini is one of Italy's most versatile and influential designers. Trained as an architect, he is particularly well known for his work in furniture and industrial design. The new forms for objects of contemporary technology and furniture that he developed have inspired designers internationally.

Bellini, who lives and works in Milan, where he was born in 1935, was part of the remarkable emergence in the 1960s of Italy—and particularly Milan—as an important design center. The 1950s, a period of reconstruction and dramatic industrial growth, had represented the beginning of a new phase in Italian design. Unlike many countries, Italy had been relatively free of a strong manufacturing tradition and became receptive to new, experimental approaches to furniture and industrial design. It was a period of great optimism and energy. Postwar Italian design represented an alternative to the Bauhaus emphasis on function and simple geometric shapes, which had taken hold in Italy in the 1930s primarily in terms of its aesthetic ideas rather than those of its ethical programs, as elsewhere in Europe. Italian designers of the 1960s were, therefore, relatively free of the limiting aspects of modernist dogma. The new design was exciting in its use of highly seductive sculptural forms, its sense of humor, and its diverse and often conflicting aesthetic approaches.[1]

The international prominence of Italian design today derives from a number of factors: talented and creative designers, a tradition of craftsmanship, and open-minded and enthusiastic manufacturers of both small and large companies willing to experiment and take economic risks with new products. Furniture manufacturers such as Cassina and B & B Italia were not merely producers but formed close alliances with designers, and were actively involved in the research and development of new materials and techniques. In most Italian firms the strong commitment to producing a well-designed object, combined with this collaborative approach, has encouraged the development of the designer's personal expression and helped ensure the quality of the final product. Bellini's work exemplifies the level of excellence that has come to be associated with Italian design.

Bellini began his career at a decisive moment in the history of twentieth-century design: the transition from mechanical to microelectronic technology. During the 1960s extraordinary strides were made in the development of microelectronics; these reduced previously bulky and heavy mechanical parts to miniaturized circuitry, replacing what in the 1950s had been large enough to fill an entire room with components small enough to fit into the hand. Having no specific shape, and freed of the rigorous restraints of mechanical interdependence, microcomponents could be combined in any number of ways, thus providing designers with a unique opportunity to create new industrial forms. Bellini's work takes full advantage of the formal freedom made possible by the new technology.

His inventive forms have established an extraordinary richness and range of metaphor.

Anthropomorphic references pervade his work. One example is the "stretched membrane," which he began using in the 1960s. When "stretched" over the prominent structural parts of furniture or machines, this single enveloping material, usually of plastic or leather, resembles skin, creating sensuous curves. A recurring theme, the elastic membrane confers an expressive, sculptural character on both his furniture and his industrial products.

He seldom uses drawings, working instead through dialogue, experimentation, and touch. His ideas are realized by engineers and artisans in full-scale models that he then refines through direct physical contact. Unlike many designers who work primarily at the drafting-board, Bellini's approach is intuitive and sensory; his concern with the way the user will experience the object contributes to its tactile and sculptural quality. It is only after his design is final that a draftsman's technical drawing is made.

Bellini's earliest work is experimental, elegant, dramatic, and often poetic, softened with curvilinear lines and anthropomorphic features. Since the 1970s his designs have become more geometric and rational. But throughout all his work, his tactile Mediterranean sensibility, along with his respect for the materials and classical forms of traditional Italian culture, have exerted a profound influence.

While Bellini's designs are interrelated, for clarity of discussion they have been divided into two groups, industrial design and furniture. Since much of his recent work is a refinement of his early products, design developments are presented chronologically within each category. This publication is not intended as a comprehensive survey of Bellini's oeuvre, but rather as a compendium of his most accomplished designs.

Mario Bellini graduated in architecture from the Milan Polytechnic in 1959. Like many of his contemporaries, he went directly into designing furniture and industrial products. In 1962 he won the first of seven Compasso d'Oro awards. In 1963 he became the chief industrial design consultant for the Olivetti Company, forming a relationship that continues to this day, and out of which has come much of Bellini's best work. As an independent consultant he has also designed important furniture for Cassina, B & B Italia, and Vitra; electronic equipment for Brionvega and Yamaha; and lighting for Artemide, Flos, and Erco. A number of his designs are represented in the collection of The Museum of Modern Art. In 1986 he became editor-in-chief of *Domus* magazine.

The miniaturization of electronic parts has given industrial designers new challenges that extend beyond the dictum "form follows function," long a guiding principle in twentieth-century design. Until the 1960s a designer's main task was to create a protective shell whose shape echoed the configuration of the machine's internal components. One of the best examples of this treatment is the Lexikon 80 office typewriter, designed in 1947 by Marcello Nizzoli, Olivetti's design consultant from the 1930s through the

MARCELLO NIZZOLI
LEXIKON 80 TYPEWRITER. 1947

1950s. A highly expressive piece, its sculptural form softens the mass of mechanisms it encloses.

The 1960s was an important experimental and formative period for Bellini. Because rapid advancements in technology and increasing miniaturization rendered business equipment obsolete shortly after manufacture, he treated each product as a design in itself rather than as part of a search for a single style. These early designs for Olivetti and Brionvega are of a different generation than his later work: at the time they were done, electronic parts were still bulky enough that their forms reflected the internal divisions of the machine.

By the early 1970s the disassociation between encasement and mechanism meant that electronic equipment could be designed regardless of the internal elements: in fact, the external form could even determine the arrangement of internal components. This had a decisive impact on product design. The designer, who had fewer restraints than ever before, was challenged with deciding the most appropriate form to give the machine.

Now that the Bauhaus ideals and aesthetics are no longer the guiding principles, there is no single aesthetic expression that can be applied to products of technology. On what criteria should the designer base decisions? According to Bellini, "machine design is now seen as a single operation whose purpose is to produce a complete object: to define a service to man within any given context of the work environment...to include the notion of a system integrated with man's environment."[2] Nevertheless, although the design of office equipment is preeminently practical, the variety of possible solutions to the same problem suggests that the design will ultimately be more influenced by aesthetic preferences.

Despite the fact that miniaturization has allowed companies and designers more flex-

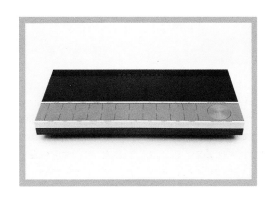

JAKOB JENSEN
BEOMASTER 6000 AMPLIFIER. 1974

MARIO BELLINI
DIVISUMMA 18 ELECTRONIC PRINTING CALCULATOR. 1972

ibility in their designs than has ever been possible, it is ironic that today many products tend to look alike. Anonymous black-box shells have become stylized solutions and are used indiscriminately to encase calculators, flashlights, and cigarette lighters. The ubiquitous black color, which implies seriousness and professionalism, is intended to give them credibility. Often the designs have little or no relation to the functioning of the objects, and offer no visible clue to their operation or purpose. They exemplify the increasing trend of our technological society toward a loss of contact with the object: there is little to which a human being can respond.

Two very different psychological attitudes toward twentieth-century products are represented by Bellini's Divisumma calculator, designed in 1972, and Jakob Jensen's elegant stereo equipment for the Danish firm of Bang & Olufsen. Bang & Olufsen sound equipment is intentionally discreet in appearance, communicating as little as possible about its function: as high-precision equipment, it is not meant to be handled. The unarticulated controls disappear into the overall design, creating a sleek, impenetrable object. The design conveys the message

"do not touch," in contrast to Bellini's calculator, which emphasizes the sensual and tactile.

Bellini emphasizes the tactile experience, for he feels adults should explore the environment through their senses, like children. He makes industrial products desirable by taking advantage of the expressive capabilities of such new materials as plastic, which lends itself to smooth, sculptural shapes, and can be formed into stretched membranes, evoking sensuous landscapes or the human body. Even though the anthropomorphic references in his work may not be immediately recognizable, they stimulate an emotional response.

Changes in model-making materials may have contributed to Bellini's shift from curvilinear to more rational and angular designs. Through the 1960s many models were of clay, a malleable material traditionally used by sculptors that lends itself to an instinctual rather than an intellectual approach. In the 1970s, when Bellini began using polystyrene, a rigid foam material cut with a heated wire, many of his designs became more geometric. Nevertheless, his intention—to make machines easily accessible—remained the same even though the par-

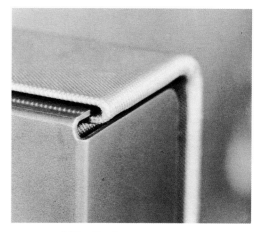

CMC7, DETAIL OF FOLDED "SKIN-PLATE"

ABOVE AND RIGHT: CMC7 MAGNETIC CHARACTER ENCODER. 1963

ticulars of his design approach changed.

From the mid-1970s the format and size of office machines ranging from sophisticated word processors to portable typewriters remained basically unchanged. Technological advances resulted in only subtle modifications in the basic shape of machines. Several of Bellini's designs for office equipment have been for products that were the first of their kind: their emblematic forms have become a standard for typewriters, calculators, and computers and have inspired numerous imitations.

The first machine Bellini designed was the **CMC7 MAGNETIC CHARACTER ENCODER.** The objective was to combine into a visually coherent shape a standard Olivetti calculating machine and a "beam" along which bank checks travel to be encoded. Bellini placed the "beam" horizontally across the top of the body. Its pristine shape

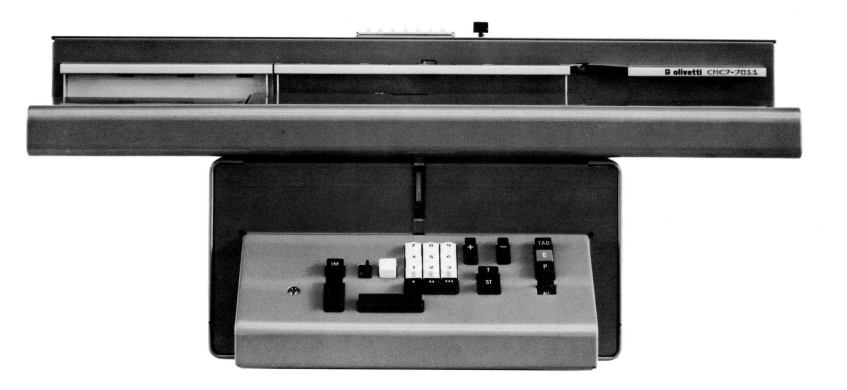

and detailing are the result of the technique he developed to form the "skin plate," a metal sheet coated with plastic. Lengths of "skin plate" are cut, bent, and folded into separate elements. These individual pieces are arranged into a system of interlocking units requiring no screws. When assembled, they create beautifully finished, smooth surfaces. The folded ends conceal unsightly raw edges and give the machine a refined look. By introducing a new technique

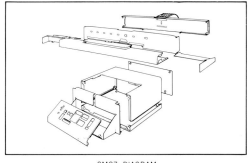

CMC7, DIAGRAM

and new material, Bellini transformed a rather simple volume into an elegant structure.

Bellini's next project for Olivetti was the PROGRAMMA 101, the first electronic desktop computer. He wanted to express a completely new machine, one that reflected new technology. His principal concern was that the computer have a look of order and simplicity, making it less intimidating and its operation visually comprehensible. The card slot is placed on cen-

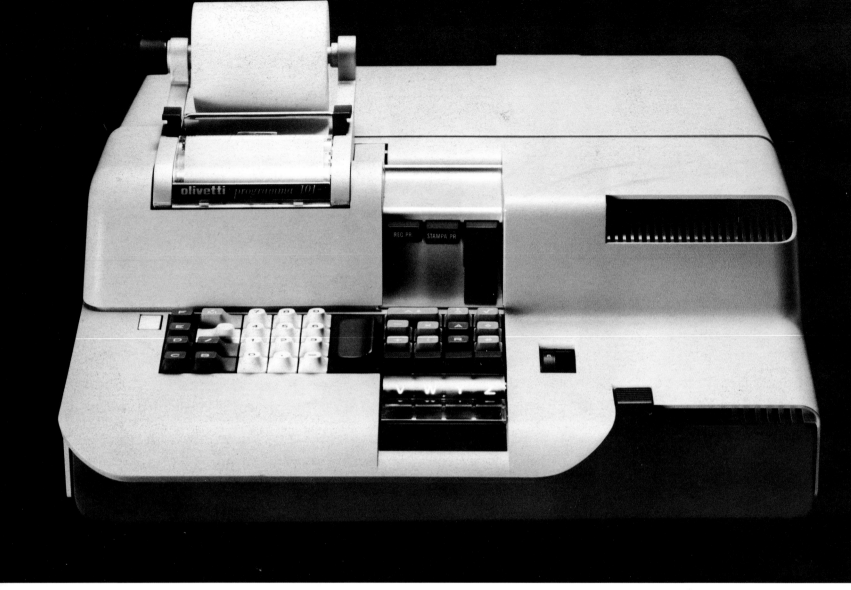

ABOVE AND RIGHT: P 101 ELECTRONIC DESKTOP COMPUTER. 1965

ter axis to give prominence to the new magnetic card feature, which activates and programs the computer. In order to place the keyboard in a comfortable relationship with the operator, Bellini lowered the form with a "tongue," which serves as a mantel, or table. It also functions as a guard rail for the magnetic card. The subtle modulations suggest the way the machine is to be used. Cast aluminum lends itself to smooth

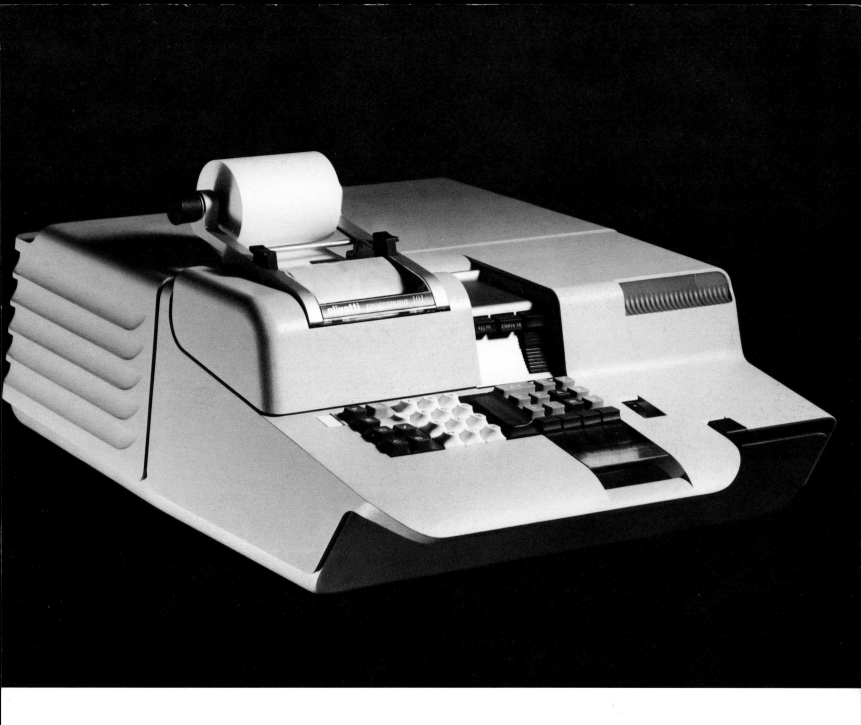

P 101, INTERNAL MECHANISMS

organic shapes, and Bellini's masterful handling of it enlivens the front and side planes, giving the computer the appearance of a living organism. Cooling vents on the side evoke fish gills; cuts for the light indicator on the upper right suggest an eye; and the handrest resembles a tongue. What could easily have been an uninteresting box becomes organic sculpture full of anthropomorphic references.

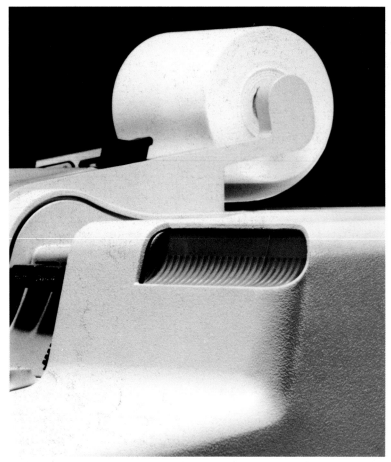

P 101, DETAIL

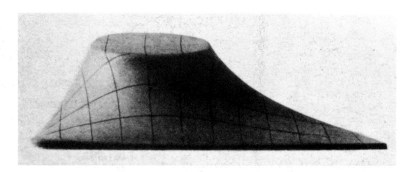

P 101, KEY, STUDY MODEL FOR STRETCHED MEMBRANE

P 101, KEYBOARD

Bellini's first use of a stretched membrane for modeling was in the design of the keys for the P 101. The challenge was to integrate the square base of the key with the circular finger area. Since there is no geometric formula that can unify the two shapes, Bellini joined them using a stretched membrane. Behaving like a soap bubble, the plastic membrane assumes a very natural and gentle passage when stretched between the square and circular perimeters. What seems like a small detail is an essential feature: the keys are the points of contact between the machine and the user. Their organic shape is pleasing to both the eye and the hand.

One of the most unusual and innovative of

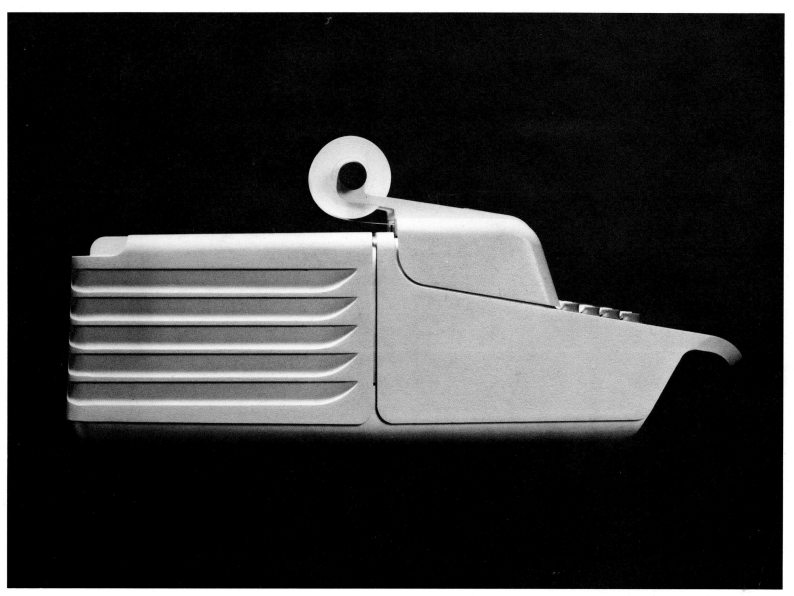

P 101, SIDE VIEW

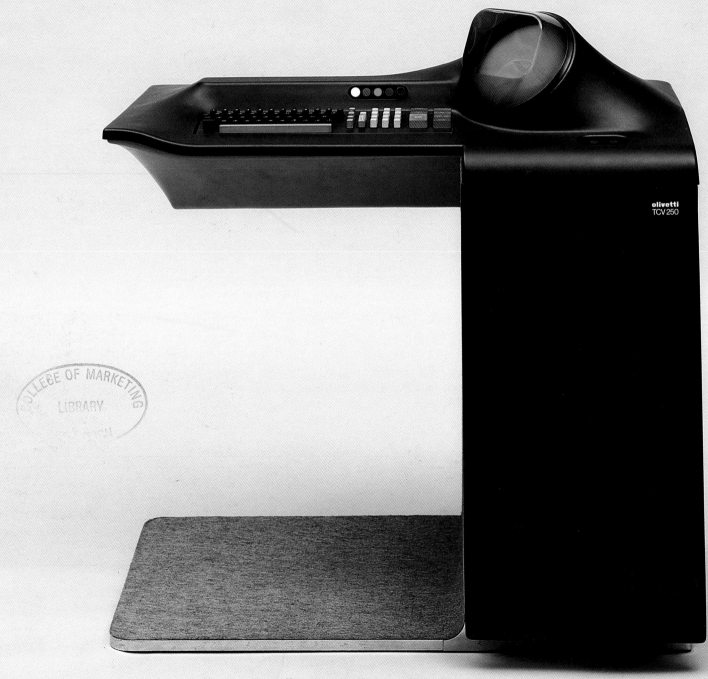

TCV 250 VIDEO DISPLAY TERMINAL. 1966

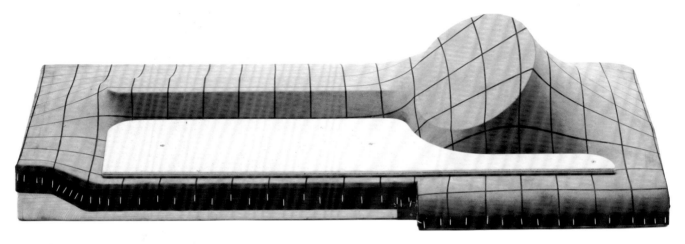

TCV 250, STUDY MODEL FOR STRETCHED MEMBRANE

CHARLES EAMES
CHAISE. 1948

Bellini's products is the **TCV 250 VIDEO DISPLAY TERMINAL**, designed for Olivetti in 1966. The objective was to organize the various elements comprising the terminal: a slanted keyboard, a sloped and cylindrical video screen, pushbuttons, and stacks of circuit boards. Elaborating on the stretched membrane used for the keys on the P 101 computer, but this time on a much larger scale, Bellini designed a continuous surface to unify the separate components. The membrane is made using a vacuum-forming process: a sheet of PVC plastic is heated and laid over a mold. When air is sucked from the underside, the plastic cools, assuming the shape of the mold. The elastic membrane, based on a tension structure, evokes tent forms.

Although the video terminal was not specified as a work station, Bellini found the components too large and cumbersome for a desktop machine, and designed it as a free-standing table. The cantilevered structure, which has fascinated many twentieth-century architects and

KEY FROM THE P 101 ELECTRONIC DESKTOP COMPUTER. 1965

LANCIA BETA DASHBOARD. 1977-78

designers, is used here to accentuate the continuous surface—a particularly voluptuous floating landscape. The terminal also has a science-fiction aspect and conveys much of the experimental mood of the 1960s. The video screen bulges from the taut skin like a cyclops' eye or a colossal pushbutton. The pushbutton, activating circuits that send machines of potentially enormous power into action, has fascinated many people and has become a metaphor for power and technology. Formally, the terminal recalls organic sculpture from the 1940s and 1950s or, for example, the experimental stressed-skin chaise designed in 1948 by Charles Eames. The piece remains a curiosity, for no one has designed anything else like it. It is not so unusual to find such a radical design coming from a young designer, but what is surprising is to find an established company like Olivetti producing the work.

Fiat commissioned Bellini in 1977 to design a new interior for an existing LANCIA BETA automobile. Although done a decade later, its mysterious space-age character relates it to the video display terminal. Made in black polyurethane foam, the curved dashboard, with controls and instruments recessed in an asymmetrical dot pattern, wraps around the driver. Like pushbuttons, the dials are assigned their own holes in the control zone, psychologically enhancing the driver's feeling of importance and power.

The portable "POP" AUTOMATIC RECORD PLAYER was produced by Minerva in 1968. It is a playful object with a softly rounded casing made of white or bright orange glossy plastic. A straightforward minimalist design, it operates like a toaster. Bellini designed everything, including the internal mechanism, with his

GA 45 "POP" AUTOMATIC RECORD PLAYER. 1968

"TOTEM" STEREO SYSTEM WITH DETACHABLE SPEAKERS. 1970

brother and frequent collaborator, Dario.

The influence of minimal sculpture can be seen in a number of Bellini's designs, the two most striking examples being the "Totem" Stereo of 1970 and the "Triangular" Television prototype he developed for Brionvega in 1968. The "Totem," designed as a cube, divides into three units. The bottom half contains all the operating devices, including a turntable and cassette recorder; the upper portion consists of two speaker units that privot from the corner and can be removed. The black circles of the speakers provide abstract, rhythmic accents. When closed, the enigmatic cube might fit anywhere in the home. The stereo unit was not a success in the marketplace, perhaps because it was introduced at a time when public preference was for individual components that could be stacked and rearranged at will.

The startling effect of the television derives from the triangular shape. The form was chosen to make the television appear less massive. But

"TRIANGULAR" TELEVISION, TOP VIEW

"TRIANGULAR" TELEVISION, PROJECT. 1968

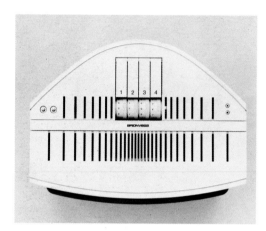

"ASTER 20" TELEVISION, TOP VIEW

what at first appears to be a rigid triangular form, takes on a surprisingly organic quality with sides that gently swell. It combines both soft and curved volumes with sharp, clean lines; the softness is contained within the rigid frame. A freestanding unit, it is intended to be seen from all sides.

Bellini's most refined product for Brionvega is the "ASTER 20" TELEVISION. The body is divided in half and can be tilted into three different positions. All the components, controls, and antenna have been arranged in an elegant abstract form. The back is as compelling as the front: its staccato dot pattern is a poetic gesture. Carefully contrived ventilation slots and holes lighten the mass, making it seem less solid and ominous.

The office machines Bellini designed for Olivetti in the 1970s were determined less by the fixed arrangement of mechanical parts than by the functional requirements of the machine's operator. The LOGOS 50/60 ELECTRONIC PRINTING CALCULATOR that he designed in 1972 derives from a traditional lectern, a proven form.

"ASTER 20" TELEVISION. 1968

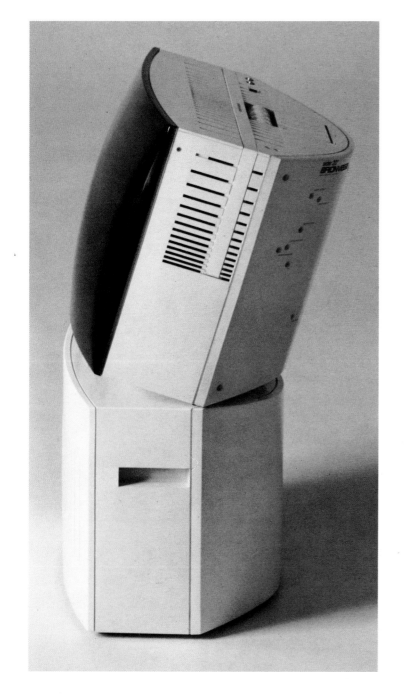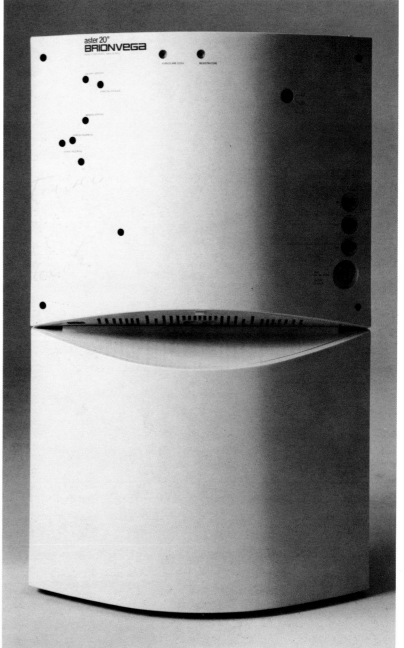

ABOVE AND RIGHT: LOGOS 50/60 ELECTRONIC PRINTING CALCULATOR. 1972

Its wedge shape has influenced much subsequent design for office equipment.

After studying the configurations he could make with the separate components of the Logos 50/60, Bellini pursued the idea of a horizontal format with the keyboard on the right and the printer to the left, the motor and power source behind. Since the keyboard was relatively flat and the printing unit high, Bellini set them in a wedge shape to keep the keyboard close to the table. The mantel he designed for the P 101 computer produced a similar result. Working closely with engineers during the initial

ABOVE AND RIGHT: LOGOS 50/60, STUDY MODELS

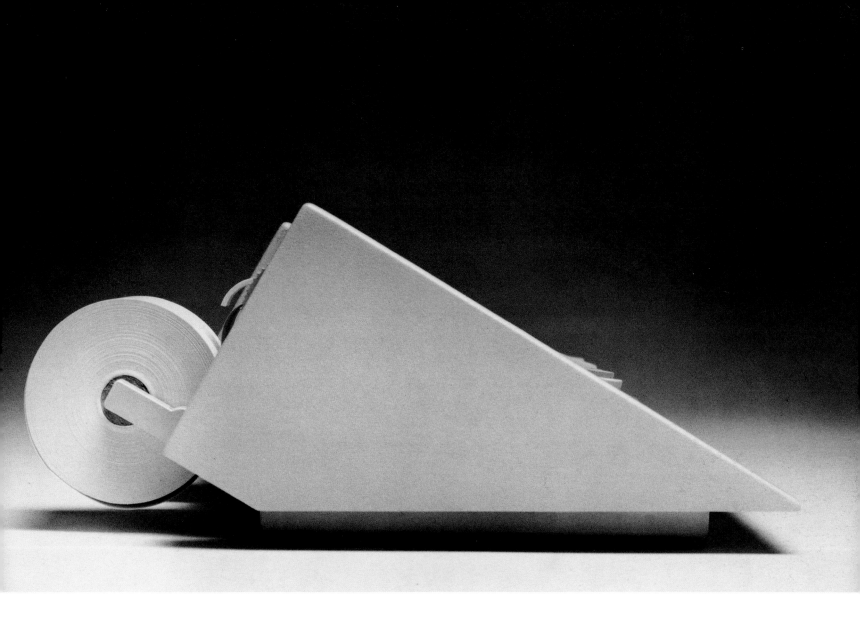

DIVISUMMA 18 ELECTRONIC PRINTING CALCULATOR. 1972

ABOVE AND RIGHT: DIVISUMMA 18, DETAILS

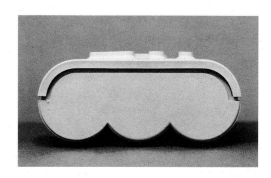

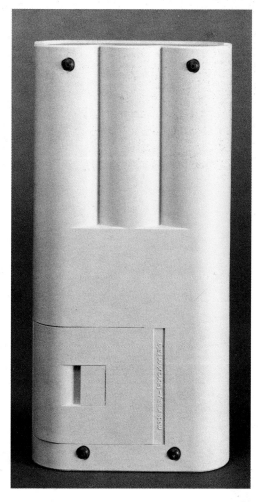

stages of development, he was able to determine the arrangement of the components. By recessing the keyboard, Bellini created a flush surface and maintained the purity of shape. The color-coded keyboard facilitates use and enhances the visual impact. The inset base makes the machine appear to hover above the table surface. The Logos 50/60 is among Bellini's most elegant designs. Its masterful form conveys the integrity and uncompromising manner with which Bellini pursues an idea, working every part to the last detail.

The DIVISUMMA 18 ELECTRONIC PRINTING CALCULATOR, designed in 1972, is a particularly persuasive alternative to the impersonal quality of most technological objects. Because the calculator is portable and intended to be hand-held, Bellini personalized it through an inventive use of form and materials. What is especially intriguing about this calculator is the continuous flexible, rubber-skin keyboard, a variation on the stretched membrane. The skin, which protects the machine from dust, is anthropomorphically suggestive. Articulated pushbuttons, covered with the soft rubber skin, are like nipples. Here the emphasis is not on calculating and power, but on stimulating a sense of pleasure. Emotive responses are not usually associated with adding machines, yet this is an irresistible artifact. One cannot help but want to hold it, touch it, play with it. The yellow color enhances the element of playfulness.

The DIVISUMMA 28 ELECTRONIC PRINTING CALCULATOR was developed at the same time as the Divisumma 18. Their casings and flexible rubber keyboards are similar, but their forms are different, as the Divisumma 28 was designed as a tabletop machine. Because of the way it was to be used, Bellini gives prominence to the inclined

ABOVE AND RIGHT: DIVISUMMA 28 ELECTRONIC PRINTING CALCULATOR. 1972

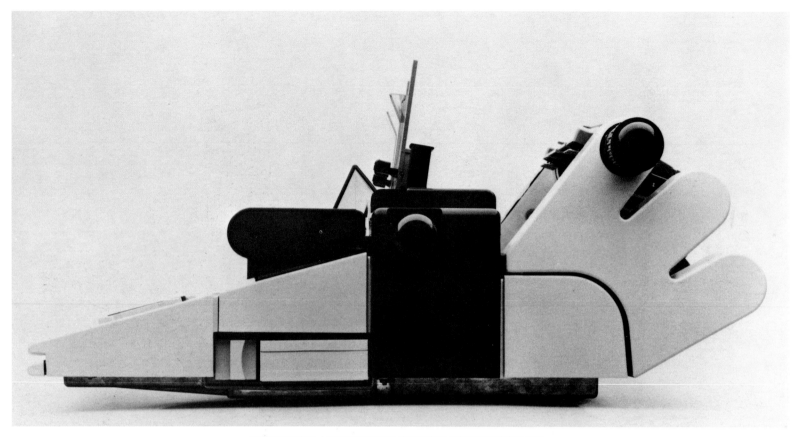

ABOVE AND RIGHT: A 4 PROGRAMMABLE ACCOUNTING-INVOICING MACHINE. 1973

A 4, DETAILS

keyboard, derived from the Logos 50/60. The Divisumma 18 and 28 were produced for only a brief period, perhaps because at the time their designs were too provocative for widespread public acceptance. In addition, the procedure for embedding plastic letters and numbers into the rubber keys was technically so complicated

they were also very expensive to produce.

One of the most unusual and structurally complex products Bellini designed for Olivetti is the A 4 PROGRAMMABLE ACCOUNTING-INVOICING MACHINE. It seems almost a hybrid of his earlier machines. Using the wedge form for the core, he tried to "tame" the piece by using different

colors, shapes, and materials to designate and punctuate the various functions and operational features. The splayed plume is an optional device for sorting paper. Transformed into an animal-like creature, it is a very impressive attempt to simplify a potentially intimidating object.

ABOVE AND RIGHT: LEXIKON 82 ELECTRIC PORTABLE TYPEWRITER. 1972-73

The first portable typewriter to use a "golf ball" movable printing element was the LEXIKON 82, designed in 1972-73. To facilitate removal from the carrying case, Bellini enclosed the machine in a smooth-fitting cover with rounded sides. The two-tone colors on the keys and body sug-gest the play of light and shadow. A single bright red knob at the end of the paper roll provides a poetic accent against the beige color. The sliding carriage and fixed printing point help keep the width to a minimum.

ABOVE AND RIGHT: "MONITOR 15" TELEVISION. 1975

"MONITOR 15," DETAIL OF TOP

MARCO ZANUSO, RICHARD SAPPER
"BLACK 201" TELEVISION. 1969

Both the "MONITOR 15" TELEVISION for Brion-vega and the YAMAHA STEREO CASSETTE DECK are examples of Bellini's tendency to treat electronic appliances as precious objects. The "Monitor 15" recalls in some ways Marco Zanuso and Richard Sapper's enigmatic black-cube television, designed several years earlier for Brionvega; however, Bellini layers his cube into three zones, with the knobs, handles, and air vents conveying military precision. Both televisions are highly formal solutions. The stereo cassette deck is a direct outgrowth of the Logos 50/60 calculator. The recessed controls and their stepped modulations take on a sculpted quality. It is another exploration of pure form.

Two inventive variations on the wedge form are the TES 401 TEXT-EDITING SYSTEM and the LOGOS 80 ELECTRONIC PRINTING CALCULATOR, both of which were designed for Olivetti in 1978. To lighten the rather thick and cumbersome volume of the TES 401, Bellini treated it like abstract sculpture, separating the mass into three parts. He gives further dimension to the piece by varying the materials, texture, and colors, and by recessing the keyboard so it is flush with the surface. Similar to the TES 401, the Logos 80 calculator makes use of the split volume, which emphasizes the separation of the keyboard and printer and breaks up the visual monotony. It was a way of expressing a new product and new technology.

The rounded organic form of the LETTERA 10 PORTABLE TYPEWRITER, designed in 1976-77, is characteristic of Bellini's earlier office machines sealed in stretched membranes. The black carriage and keyboard appear as voids against the light-colored body, creating the illusion of a hollow shell. A low center of gravity is achieved by the taut skin, which clings to the table like a

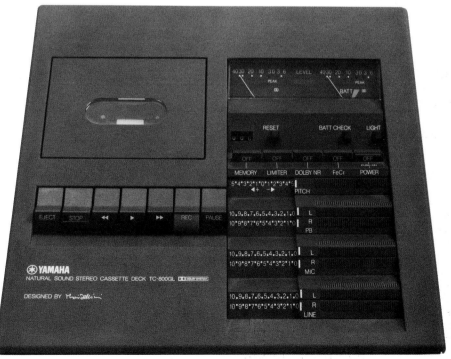

TOP AND BOTTOM: YAMAHA STEREO CASSETTE DECK. 1974

ABOVE AND RIGHT: TES 401 TEXT-EDITING SYSTEM. 1978

suction cup. This and Bellini's use of the stretched membrane for office equipment did not represent a style, but were very effective methods of achieving both unity and continuity of form. After the mid-1970s he discontinued the stretched membrane in his business machines; as computer parts became increasingly compact, it was no longer a nec-

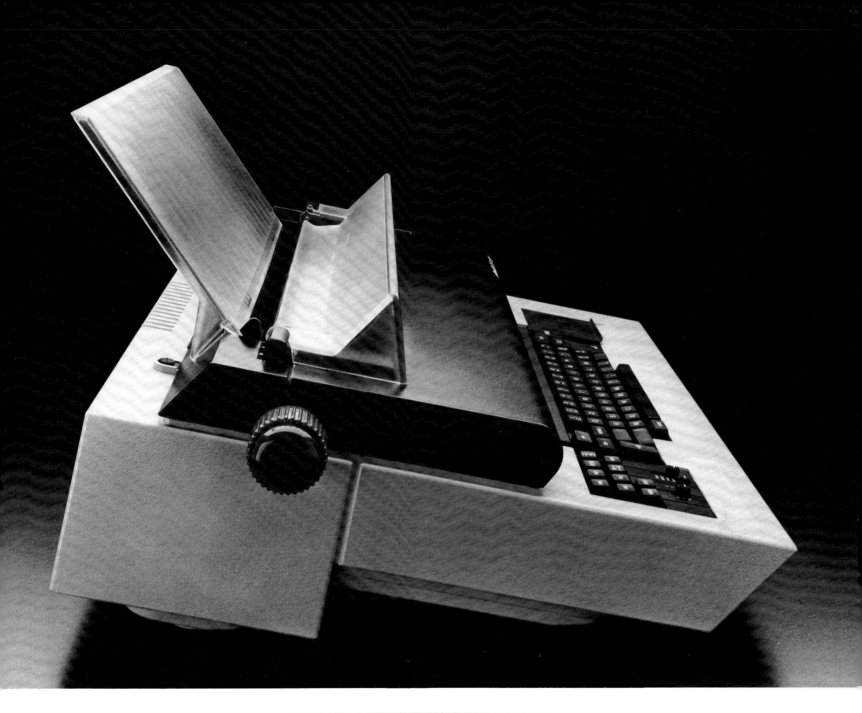

LOGOS 80 ELECTRONIC PRINTING CALCULATOR. 1978

LETTERA 10 PORTABLE TYPEWRITER. 1976-77

ET 111 ELECTRONIC TYPEWRITER. 1983

"PORTATONE" PORTABLE ELECTRONIC ORGAN. 1984

essary means of integrating the components and diminishing the bulk of the overall design.

The **ET ELECTRONIC TYPEWRITER** series and related portable Praxis series, designed for Olivetti between 1978 and 1983, are Bellini's most familiar and influential models. Their geometric forms are more businesslike in appearance than his earlier work. They have a look of precision and efficiency. Although the keyboard can often interrupt the unity of a design, Bellini kept the keys in the same black color as the rest of the machine to achieve visual coherence. The various models within the ET and Praxis series all belong to a family of typewriters that has created a strong corporate image for Olivetti. Bellini attempts to enrich the geometric form by introducing a corrugated pattern around the back and side perimeters. It is not only decorative but functional, serving as a method of both integrating the ventilation cuts and subtly modulating the surface with light and shadow. In this he was influenced by Marcello Nizzoli and Ettore Sottsass, both of whom used similar patterning on earlier designs for Olivetti.

The Olivetti Company has served as a laboratory throughout Bellini's career, giving him the freedom to experiment and to develop a repertoire of forms and tactile details that he has extended to his other design work. Bellini's insistence on refinement, elegance, and sophistication has led to a number of international commissions from companies such as Yamaha, Erco, and Zojirushi, which desire high-quality products. His designs for a television antenna, an electronic organ, a thermos, and even furniture derive from the work for Olivetti for which he had become known.

Most of Bellini's industrial designs intentionally surpress the technical dimension. How-

"ROBOT" ROTATING ANTENNA. 1980

"MINIDECA" THERMOS. 1983

TOP AND BOTTOM: "CLASS" WATER FAUCET. 1978

ever, in his most recent typewriter and his lighting fixtures for the German lighting company Erco, the structural elements are deliberately articulated to achieve a new expressive aesthetic. The "ECLIPSE" SPOTLIGHTS for Erco do not fall within the category of furniture, but rather they are specialized mechanical equipment. Their adjustability and high-tech aesthetic convey efficiency, high performance, and technical precision.

At the same time that Bellini was creating rational geometric shapes, he returned to his earlier use of sensuous sculptural forms for the "CLASS" WATER FAUCET, designed in 1978 for Ideal Standard. Less rigid than most hardware, its explicitly sexual quality is indebted to modern organic sculpture. It has a look of spontaneity not often associated with Bellini's work.

A new image for Olivetti's product line was created in 1986 with the **ETP 55 PORTABLE ELECTRONIC TYPEWRITER**. The objective was to design an inexpensive, lightweight machine that would be distinguished from Olivetti's competitors and attract a new audience. Still using the wedge form as the dominant layout, he created a completely new character by altering several features. In particular, the color change from black to a combination of gray, blue, and yellow gives the typewriter a fresh appearance. The highly articulated form expresses the most current technology, which has reduced the keyboard to a thin plane that defines the overall design. Everything else is subordinated and appears to radiate from the central paper roll,

TOP AND BOTTOM: "ECLIPSE" LOW-VOLTAGE SPOTLIGHTS. 1985

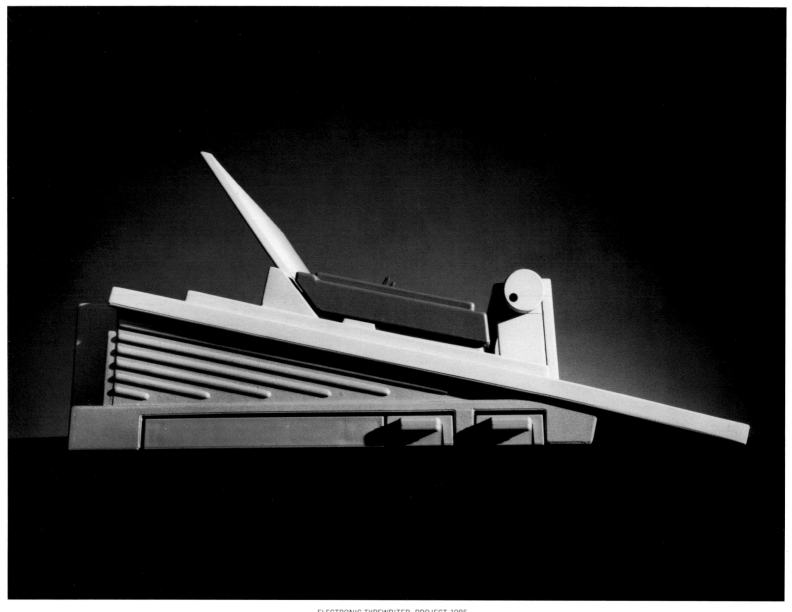

ELECTRONIC TYPEWRITER, PROJECT. 1985

which is punctuated by yellow knobs. The corrugated surface heightens the sculptural quality and gives the machine a sporty character.

The ETP 55 typewriter was strongly influenced by Bellini's studies in 1985 for the design of a highly advanced electronic typewriter. Although technical difficulties prevented the machine from being produced, its articulated design, like that of the ETP 55, represents a new direction for Bellini.

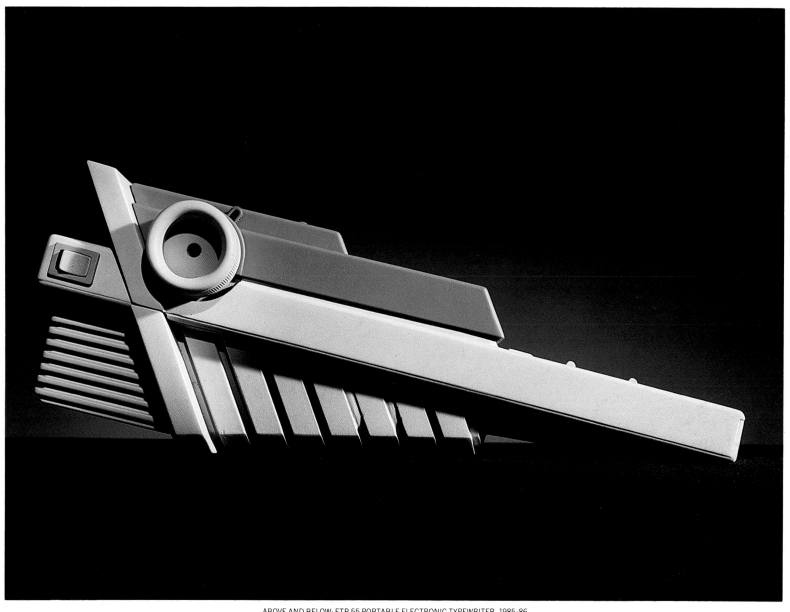

ABOVE AND BELOW: ETP 55 PORTABLE ELECTRONIC TYPEWRITER. 1985-86

Unlike office machines, which have a very short history, furniture has come to us through centuries of tradition. New designs tend to be variations of and refinements on previous examples or to reflect the introduction of new materials and technology. But while technology and materials have changed, the basic concept of the chair never changes. Bellini's inventive use of traditional and new synthetic materials and sophisticated molding techniques place him firmly among leading Italian furniture designers of the past two decades.

During the postwar reconstruction of the 1950s the emphasis was on economy of materials and lightness, and clarity and understated design prevailed. Designers became preoccupied with the thin line, and sought to use wood and metal with the thinnest diameter possible. Influenced by furniture from Scandinavia and America, particularly the work of Charles Eames, the Italians—most notably Franco Albini and Gio Ponti—were especially successful in their use of minimal material. Their furniture appeared fragile, almost as if it would blow away.

But the public's preference for comfort combined with the counterculture movement in the latter part of the 1960s encouraged less formality in many aspects of living, including ways of sitting, contributing to the change in character of Italian furniture. The Thirteenth Triennale of 1964 in Milan, based on the theme of leisure time, anticipated this new sensibility. Predicated on the notion of new materials and techniques, padded, flexible furniture presented as voluminous sculptural shapes became the dominant image. The flexible, overstuffed construct represented a dramatic shift from the Bauhaus predilection for the linear and planar, for furniture stripped down to its essentials. The emphasis was no longer on purity, thinness, or refinement.

Instead, Bellini and other Italian designers drew inspiration from the natural world, science fiction, and Minimal and Pop art. Many of the changes in the formal character of furniture reflected new directions in modern sculpture. Both artists and designers celebrated popular culture by making mundane objects highly visible, transforming them into humorous, oversized constructs. Claes Oldenburg's bulky soft sculptures, which are flexible and can assume various positions, had a particular influence on many furniture designers, including Bellini. From the mid-1960s through the mid-1970s, Bellini's padded furniture appeared to be without a rigid support structure. The ultimate in responsive seating was the "Sacco" Bean Bag Chair, designed in 1969 by Pierro Gatti, Cesare Paolini, and Franco Teodoro. A shapeless leather sack half-filled with polystyrene beads, it acquires the shape the user imposes on it and, like a sack, can be moved anywhere.

A further effect of more informal lifestyles was that flexibility took precedence over furniture with one specific use. The tendency of many Italian designers, including Bellini, was to develop seating units composed of modular elements offering a variety of compositions and uses, depending on individual needs.

CLAES OLDENBURG
FLOOR CONE. 1962

PIERRO GATTI, CESARE PAOLINI, FRANCO TEODORO
"SACCO" BEAN BAG CHAIR. 1969

The informality of furniture was achieved partly by using new materials. During the late 1960s soft substances became available in a quantity and size that allowed for furniture to be made entirely of sponge material. Injection-molded polyurethane foam, one of the most modern materials in terms of furniture production, became popular with designers. It replaced foam rubber, making possible products that were structurally more complex. An expandable material, polyurethane can assume any shape and is resilient yet firm enough to support a person.[3] It has simplified the production process: it modified structural components, eliminated the need for joints, and could assume the elastic properties of straps and springs. In 1966 C & B Italia, a partnership between Cesare Cassina and Piero Busnelli that was to last until 1973, further developed polyurethane by introducing the cold-foam process. This manufacturing technique enabled both rigid and flexible qualities to occur within the same piece of foam.[4]

Bellini's designs for both Cassina and B & B Italia (formerly C & B Italia) helped redefine the typology of padded furniture and its relation to the chair's structure. His aesthetic preference for anthropomorphic forms led him to emphasize the correspondence between the inside and the outside, the bones and the skin. His designs are not just sculptures that disregard the internal structure. The leather and fabric upholstery behaves like skin stretched in tension over generously padded frames. The "skin" serves as a containing element and works in unity with the structure, the "bones," creating a sensuous sculptural form. According to Bellini, his furniture "is not covered in fabric, it is built with it."[5]

The late 1970s were marked by a historicizing mood among architects and designers. Many of their efforts to retrieve the past culminated in designs typified by an assemblage of forms, often poorly integrated and frequently of an ephemeral nature. Bellini's response has been to reappraise traditional furniture forms and their symbolic references. This work does not rely on new materials and techniques to generate new typologies, but rather makes use of strong, enduring forms.

Beginning in 1976 Bellini developed, in collaboration with Cassina, a collection of furniture systems called "The Book of Furniture." Well-designed, superbly crafted furniture derived from traditional and elemental forms was realized in a series of variations. In contrast to the curvilinear, padded, and "dressed" character of much of Bellini's work, these pieces are very pure, rational, and formal. Based on similar proportions, manufacturing process, and details, the furniture units can be combined and regrouped in any number of ways to suit the needs of the individual and the living space. Unlike some of his earlier furniture, these monolithic slabs and cubes can be deduced from drawings.

A few months after graduating from architectural school, Bellini received a commission to design his first piece of furniture. He created a plywood table using a minimum of material. Consisting of four U-shaped leg elements and a square surface, the combined parts formed a thin membrane. The legs and tabletop are not solid, but are defined by the meeting of planes. Refined by virtue of the delicacy of the piece and corner joints, it is a diagram of the basic table form.

LE CORBUSIER, PIERRE JEANNERET, CHARLOTTE PERRIAND
"FAUTEUIL GRAND CONFORT, PETIT MODÈLE" EASY CHAIR. 1928

In 1965 Bellini designed for Cassina the **"932"** CHAIR, based on the theme of a cube. Reducing a traditional armchair to a backrest, seat, and armrest, the "932" single-seat version is composed of four huge upholstered foam cushions secured by a wide belt. It derives from Le Corbusier's "Grand Confort" easy chair of 1928, which consists of four large, loose cushions fitting within a tubular steel frame. In this piece Le Corbusier ingeniously brought the steel structure from the inside to the outside. Bellini's chair was one of the first to be produced without any rigid internal or external frame and to completely dispense with legs. The "932" chair was a modular system in which cushions were treated like building blocks and could be arranged to form a one-, two-, or three-seat chair by adding further cushions and putting a longer belt around them.

TABLE, 1960

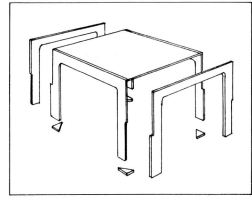

TABLE, DIAGRAM

"932/2" ARMCHAIR, SINGLE-SEAT VERSION. 1965

"AMANTA" MODULAR LOUNGE CHAIR. 1966

It resembles Minimal sculpture one can sit on. A new and unique feature of Bellini's design is the "belt." The notion of "dressed" furniture, which is peculiar to his work, is a recurring theme throughout his career.

An ideal material for mass-production, plastic can be used in the condition in which it leaves the steel molds. Because it can be made in great quantities, one of its principal applications has been for low-cost furniture. Bellini's earliest experiment with plastic was for the "AMANTA" LOUNGE CHAIR, developed in 1966 at C & B Italia's Research and Development Center. It is composed of two parts: padded cushions and an L-shaped hard plastic shell of polyester-reinforced fiberglass molded in one continuous form without any sharp corners. As with the "932" chair, Bellini put the structure on the outside to hold the cushions in place.

The "Amanta" is a practical piece of furniture. What makes it especially appealing is the expanse of the glossy plastic membrane. Bellini took advantage of the fluid character of plastic to create a seductive sculptural form. An interesting feature is the slit down the center back. It was added to later versions to increase resilience without sacrificing strength. Like the spherical rubber feet, it maximizes elasticity and lightens the mood of the chair. Later variations include an armchair, brightly colored plastic shells, and for those who resist plastic, a completely upholstered version.

The idea of making a chair in one piece of one substance has challenged many twentieth-century designers. The "TENERIDE" OFFICE CHAIR represents Bellini's experimental use of polyurethane both as a shape and as a finishing surface. Developed at the Centro Cassina in 1970, the accordionlike chair was made from a

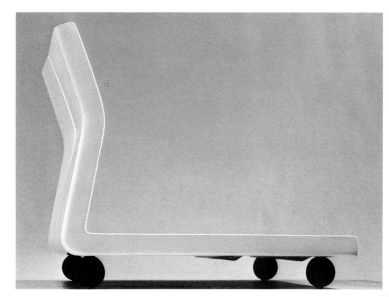

"AMANTA," SHELL

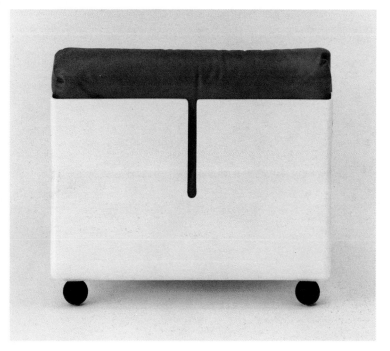

"AMANTA," BACK VIEW

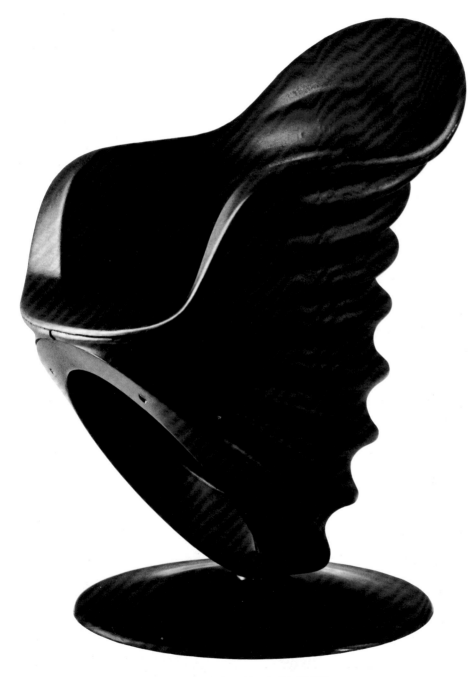

"TENERIDE" OFFICE CHAIR, PROJECT. 1970

single piece of integral "self-skinning" poly-urethane, a tough, self-sealing material currently used for dashboards and motorcycle seats. The finished surface eliminated the need for uphol-stery. By combining this form with resilient poly-urethane, Bellini sought to express the notion of flexibility associated with office chairs. Like a live organism, the caterpillar shape not only sug-gests movement, but allows the chair to flex. "Teneride" never entered production. Aside from any technical difficulties, its *2001* refer-ence was perhaps too futuristic for market acceptance. An additional problem was strong public resistance to a synthetic material that was not particularly pleasing to the touch. Nonethe-less, it represents a fascinating example of a company's willingness to let a designer search for new forms.

Bellini's experiments with manipulating single materials extended to his lamp designs. The "CHIARA" FLOOR LAMP represents the transfor-mation of a sheet of shiny stainless steel into a cylindrical light sculpture. The light source, hid-den in the base, creates a luminous well capped by a hood, evocative of a nun's habit. Like most of Bellini's products, the drawings were made after the design was developed from paper cutouts.

The "AREA" series of floor and ceiling lamps recalls organic forms Bellini created with the stretched membrane. In contrast to many of the sophisticated halogen lamps being produced at the time, in these simple pieces Bellini explores the effect of light-diffusing material. Most suc-cessful as a hanging lamp, the molded cloth is a poetic gesture of light and cloth frozen in movement.

With the "STELLE" ARMCHAIR, Bellini wanted to create a lightweight, padded furnishing con-

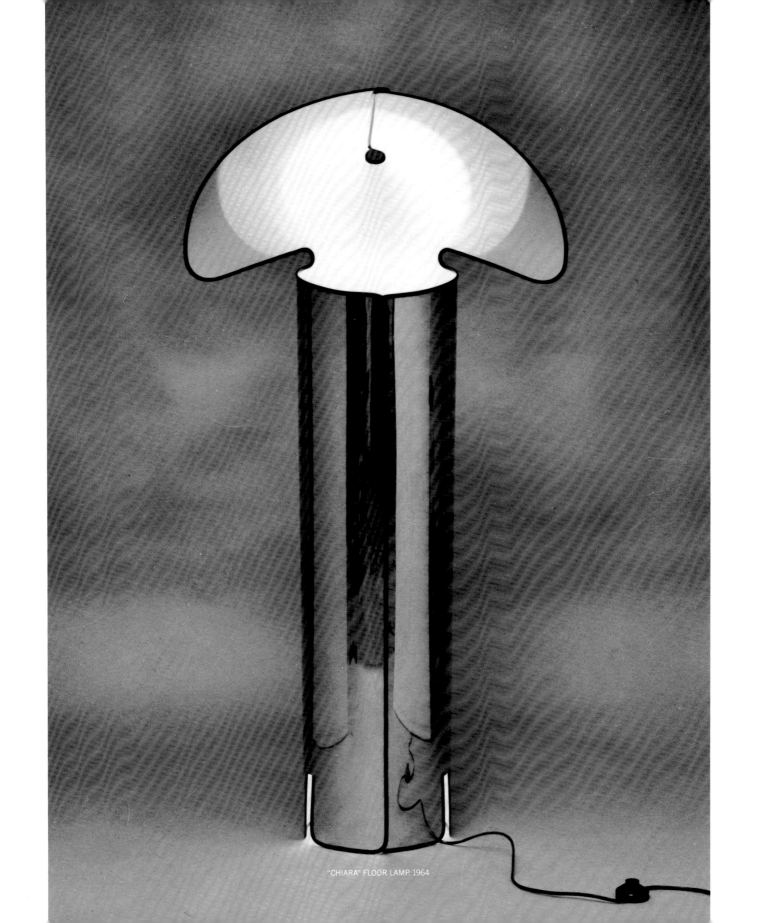

"CHIARA" FLOOR LAMP. 1964

"AREA" HANGING LAMP. 1974

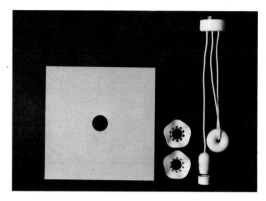

"AREA" COMPONENTS.

sisting of mass-produced parts that the factory could easily store and assemble without compromising the chair's comfort. Unlike traditional seating, in which the structural elements are joined to form a solid frame, this piece is held together by a balance of tension. The foldable frame is composed of three U-shaped tubular steel units secured with hinges. Bellini compared the structure to the "light frame of a pair of eyeglasses."[6] Polyurethane-foam padding is anchored to the back and armrests, and the Dacron-filled cushions are attached to the upholstery. The chair is "dressed" and held together with a quilted cover equipped with zippers. As opposed to the "Bambole," the parts are articulated, softened with padding.

The **"Bambole" Armchair** was designed to be a leisure chair suited to the new casual lifestyle. A piece of overstuffed, soft furniture, it wraps itself around the sitter. Bellini wanted a flexible and resilient chair, without a rigid supporting structure, that would renew its original shape after use. The intention was to create the effect of a swollen pillow resting on the floor by filling the "Bambole" with foam-rubber pellets.

"LE STELLE" ARMCHAIR. 1974

However, sufficiently durable foam pellets did not exist in the early 1970s, and within a few months of use the chair collapsed. The Research Center consequently developed a cold-foam molded "cushion" of varying densities that could create both firm corners and a supple seat and back.

The structure of the "Bambole" consisted of four different cold-foams mixed in differing proportions. A thick and hard foam used for the base became softer and springier toward the seat and upper edges. A tubular metal insert, immersed in the foam, gave the chair additional support. Dacron padding was attached to the seat and back structure and remained hidden below the upholstery, approximating the plump form Bellini originally intended. Molded as one large polyurethane cushion with no apparent structure, the "Bambole" contributed to the new image of the overstuffed armchair. The shape, however, is more controlled than in other pieces of Italian soft furniture. The "Bambole" was available as both single- and multiple-seating units.

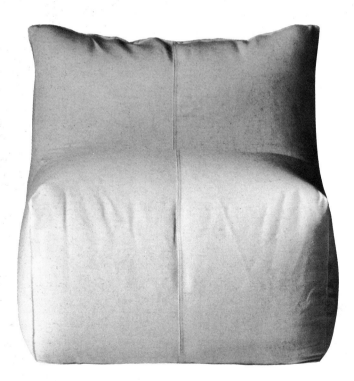

"LE BAMBOLE" SIDE CHAIR. 1972

"LE BAMBOLE" ARMCHAIR. 1972

"LE BAMBOLE" SOFA. 1972

"CAB" SIDE CHAIR. 1976

"CAB" SIDE CHAIR, LEG DETAIL

One of the most original pieces of furniture of the last fifteen years is the **"CAB" SIDE CHAIR** that Bellini designed in 1976 with Cassina's Centro Design e Comunicazione. The chair was conceived without any sketches. Bellini began with a technically simple welded-steel frame reduced to the essential components: four legs, a seat, and a back. He "dressed" the chair entirely in leather, zipped together at the legs like boots. It is an upholstered armature. Concealing the structure adds an element of mystery, representing an inversion of the Bauhaus preoccupation with revealing the way an object is made. The leather skin gives it a soft, anthropomorphic quality and one is not quite sure how the chair is supported. The character of this piece is determined by the leather. The stitching along the

"CAB" ARMCHAIR, BACK DETAIL

seams is left exposed to give the chair a sense of richness and craftsmanship. The whole piece obtains a finesse through subtle details. Nothing can be added or taken away without compromising the overall effect of the piece.

Of even greater elegance is the armchair version. The structure for the armrest was achieved by extending the front legs up past the seat. "Dressed" in one continuous leather membrane, the passage between the front and back armature does not follow the form of the underlying structure but assumes its own route, creating a very serene landscape. This version takes particular advantage of leather's rigid yet pliable character, which superimposes its sculptural qualities on the overall appearance of the chair. One is not aware of the supporting frame. In

"CAB" ARMCHAIR. 1978

addition to the side and armchair, this series includes a settee and, more recently, a lounge version with cushions.

Bellini's "TENTAZIONI" seating series, designed for Cassina in 1973, was a further effort to give a new image to the conventional armchair. A rigid and upright chair, it is less casual in appearance than the "Bambole." The difference in character is a result of the structure: all the components are fixed, yet still flexible, held together in tension. Bellini has on occasion described the tension as analogous "to the cords of a boxing ring." Like the "Bambole," the upholstery is no longer just a covering but has an interdependent relation with the internal structure, which determines how the material will behave. In comparison to the way foam rubber is traditionally encased, the upholstery on the "Tentazioni" is an important containing structural element. Like most of Bellini's designs, this chair is a result of the extraordinary craftsmanship still available in Italy today.

"TENTAZIONI" DINING CHAIR. 1973

"BREAK" DINING CHAIR. 1976

"BREAK" ARMCHAIR, PANEL DETAIL

The **"Break" Dining Chair** belongs to the family of modular furniture systems Bellini developed with Cassina for "The Book of Furniture." The principle is that additive panels can be assembled in an endless variety of arrangements and uses. Its schematic quality relates it to the basic idea of what a chair looks like. The expandable panel system and the reduction to essential elements recall Bellini's "932" chair. However, the "Break" represents a shift from generously padded furniture to a more architectural image with rigid planar surfaces. The thin panels are made of "self-skinning" injected polyurethane foam. Unlike wood, this material permits resiliency along the armrests. Bellini strives for a combination of rigid and flexible that is not visible; the chair appears to be firm, but when touched it yields unexpectedly, behaving in a soft way. Again Bellini aims for an element of surprise, of discovery. This contrast is even more subtle than, for example, the "Triangular" television because the "Break" chair has elements

"IL COLONNATO" TABLE. 1977

that move in relation to the human body. This chair demonstrates Bellini's concern for craftsmanship, which he extends to every detail. The stitched piping along the edge emphasizes the vertical outline. The zipper, important as both a functional element and a finishing detail, connects the panels, allowing for a coherent, expandable system.

The "COLONNATO" TABLE was also designed for Cassina's "The Book of Furniture." Its elemental form of neoclassical provenance is reduced to planes of varying shapes, sizes, and materials resting on supports evocative of columns. Its architectural quality is reminiscent of basic temple structures. Bellini's inspiration for the table was Stonehenge, which he considers one of the most fundamental expressions of architecture. The design does not depend on any new technology but relies on the sumptuous use of marble, a traditional material. The luxurious, high-level finish of marble represents the sensuous quality of materials to which Bellini responds. With the delicate wood table he designed in 1960, his concern was to conserve material; here it was to celebrate it. Although the design of large marble tables is not new, the "Colonnato" is modern in that the position and number of legs are not fixed and can be rearranged at will.

Bellini's elegant designs for a series of exhibition vitrines demonstrate his versatility. In 1983 he was commissioned to design display cases for the exhibition "The Treasury of San Marco," which the Olivetti Company organized for international tour. The simple pyramid structure, when elevated on four columns, takes on a jewelbox quality, emphasizing the preciousness of the sacred artifact it houses. Each vitrine is equipped with its own light source, attached to

"THE TREASURY OF SAN MARCO" EXHIBITION VITRINE. 1983-84

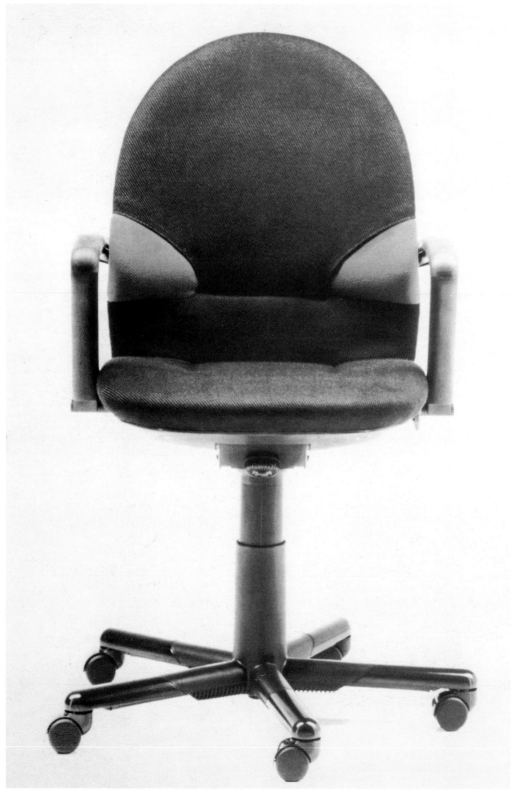

"PERSONA" OFFICE CHAIR. 1979-84

the corners and apex of the pyramid. The angled glass facilitates closer examination. Designed as free-standing units, the objects can be viewed from all four sides.

From 1979 to 1984 Bellini developed a group of office chairs in cooperation with Vitra, a leading Swiss manufacturer of office seating. The aggressive appearance of many office chairs is often a deliberate attempt to impress the consumer with the chair's many adaptable features. However, Bellini designed the "Persona" and "Figura" chairs with the same sensitivity and finesse with which he approached many of his machines for Olivetti—he wanted to "tame" them, to make them more appealing and less machinelike. The names of his chairs are not coincidental.

The "PERSONA" is Bellini's most technically sophisticated chair. The system of internal gears and mechanisms, which adjust automatically to the body's natural movements, were developed in collaboration with Vitra during a five-year period. The exposed plastic shell recalls the "Amanta" chair of 1966, but the contoured form reveals its function as an office chair. Without being aggressive, it has a look of efficiency.

"PERSONA" OFFICE CHAIR, BACK DETAIL

The "FIGURA" makes use of an existing office chair produced by Vitra, but by "dressing" it with stylish upholstery, Bellini conceals the high-tech aspect. The belt, pleat, and impeccable tailoring exemplify the Italian flair for haute couture and give the chair personality and elegance. The wide belt does not have the Pop art overtones of that on the "932" chair but rather, by its suggestion of a waist, implies movement where we normally expect it to occur in the human body. The upholstery, which is zipped together, can be removed for cleaning and change of colors.

These chairs represent an integration of Bellini's experience with both industrial and furniture design. Like his machines, they subtly express their function and are clearly defined. By treating them as "dressed" mechanisms, Bellini understates the mechanical structures and makes them more familiar to us.

Bellini was commissioned by the Indian government to participate in "The Golden Eye" exhibit, which took place in 1985 at the Cooper-Hewitt Museum in New York. The purpose was to encourage and revive the traditional Indian crafts, "updating" them to reflect contemporary western taste. Notable architects and designers from around the world were asked to submit designs that could be realized using traditional Indian craftsmanship. Bellini proposed a bench with a very simple structure carved in red sandstone, the "FORTE ROSSO." The low, deep proportions represent Bellini's effort to combine the Indian way of sitting with that of the West. The

"FIGURA" OFFICE CHAIR. 1979-84

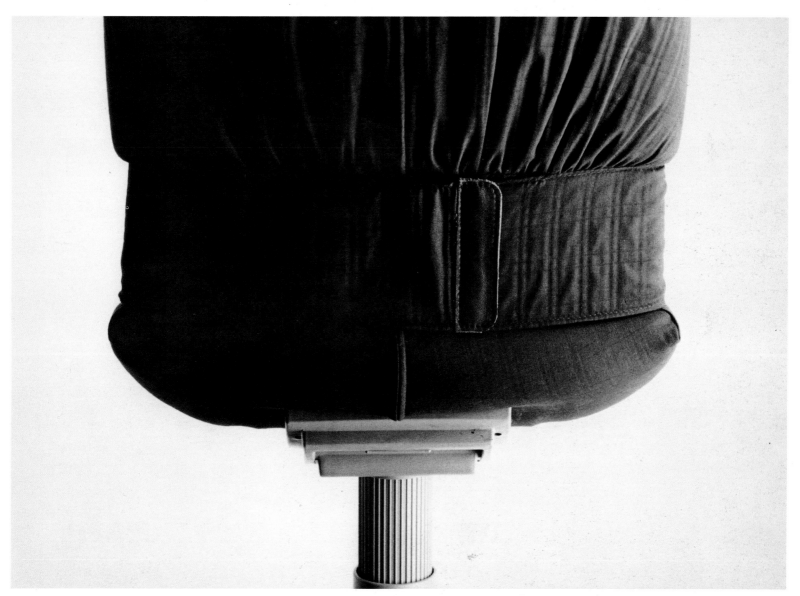

"FIGURA" OFFICE CHAIR, BACK DETAIL

"FORTE ROSSO" BENCH. 1985

corrugated surface, a deliberate functional and decorative device, is an extension of the surface treatment of his electronic typewriters. Intended for outdoor use, the corrugation is a self-cleaning feature that is weather-resistant. It also creates a rhythmic pattern that will minimize any scarring or damage to the surface. The textural pattern, along with the way the seat is set into the rigid frame, gives the bench a noble presence. It is monumental furniture for use in a public space. The strong architectural character reflects Bellini's recent return to the pursuit of architecture.

1. The achievements and ingenuity of postwar Italian design were documented by Emilio Ambasz in the exhibition "Italy: The New Domestic Landscape," organized in 1972 at The Museum of Modern Art. It provided a forum for the presentation of the diverse and often conflicting approaches that characterize contemporary Italian design.

2. Transcript of a lecture by Mario Bellini, given in the Department of Design Research, Royal College of Art, London, November 1986.

3. Mario Mastropietro, ed., *An Industry for Design: The Research Designers and Corporate Image of B & B Italia* (Milan: Edizioni Lybra Immagire s.n.c., 1986), p. 56.

4. Ibid.

5. Ibid, p. 138.

6. Ibid. p. 69.

Unless otherwise indicated, all pieces were designed by Mario Bellini and manufactured in Italy. Dimensions of works are given as height by width by depth.

Marcello Nizzoli. LEXIKON 80 TYPEWRITER. 1947. Enameled metal, 9 x 11 x 15″ (22.8 x 28 x 38.1 cm). Manufactured by Ing. C. Olivetti & C., S.p.A. The Museum of Modern Art, New York, gift of Olivetti Corporation of America.

Jakob Jensen. BEOMASTER 6000 AMPLIFIER. 1974. Steel, aluminum, and wood, 3⅛ x 26⅜ x 12½″ (8 x 67 x 31.7 cm). Manufactured by Bang & Olufsen, Denmark. The Museum of Modern Art, New York, gift of the manufacturer.

CMC7 MAGNETIC CHARACTER ENCODER. 1963. Folded "skin-plate," painted and folded sheet metal, cast-injected polypropylene, 13⁹⁄₁₆ x 33½ x 21⅛″ (34.5 x 85.4 x 53.7 cm). Manufactured by Ing. C. Olivetti & C., S.p.A. Awarded the 1964 Compasso d'Oro prize.

PROGRAMMA 101 ELECTRONIC DESKTOP COMPUTER. 1965. Die-cast aluminum body. 7½ x 18⅞ x 24″ (19 x 48 x 61 cm). Manufactured by Ing. C. Olivetti & C., S.p.A.

TCV 250 VIDEO DISPLAY TERMINAL. 1966. Vacuum-cast ABS plastic plate and sheet metal, cast-injected ABS plastic, 36⅞ x 36¹⁄₁₆ x 22″ (93.5 x 91.6 x 55.8 cm). Manufactured by Ing. C. Olivetti & C., S.p.A. The Museum of Modern Art, New York, gift of the manufacturer.

Study model for stretched membrane surface of TCV 250 VIDEO DISPLAY TERMINAL. 1966. Elastic plastic, wood. Manufactured by Ing. C. Olivetti & C., S.p.A.

Charles Eames. CHAISE (full-scale model). 1948. Prototype for stressed-skin shell; hard rubber foam between two layers of plastic, painted gray; wood and metal rod base, 32½ x 59 x 34¼″ (82.5 x 149.8 x 87 cm). The Museum of Modern Art, New York, gift of the designer.

LANCIA BETA DASHBOARD. 1977-78. ABS plastic, PVC and integral polyurethane foam, 55⅛ x 76¾ x 59¹⁄₁₆″ (140 x 195 x 150 cm). Designed in collaboration with Dario Bellini. Manufactured by Fiat Auto, S.p.A.

GA 45 "POP" AUTOMATIC RECORD PLAYER. 1968. ABS plastic body. 3⅛ x 7⅞ x 8⅝″ (8 x 20 x 22 cm). Designed in collaboration with Dario Bellini. Manufactured by Minerva, S.p.A. The Museum of Modern Art, New York, gift of the manufacturer.

"TOTEM" STEREO SYSTEM WITH DETACHABLE SPEAKERS, model RR 130. 1970. White-lacquered wood, 20½ x 20¹⁄₁₆ x 20¹⁄₁₆″ (52 x 51 x 51 cm). Designed in collaboration with Dario Bellini. Manufactured by Brionvega, S.p.A. The Museum of Modern Art, New York, gift of the manufacturer.

"TRIANGULAR" TELEVISION, project. 1968. Black-painted wood, 24 x 25¾ x 29⅞″ (61 x 65.5 x 76 cm). Designed in collaboration with Dario Bellini. Manufactured by Brionvega, S.p.A.

"ASTER 20" TELEVISION. 1968. ABS plastic body. 28⅞ x 18⅝ x 15⁷⁄₁₆″ (73.4 x 47.3 x 39.2 cm). Designed in collaboration with Dario Bellini. Manufactured by Brionvega, S.p.A.

LOGOS 50/60 ELECTRONIC PRINTING CALCULATOR. 1972. Die-cast aluminum body, ABS plastic, 4⅞ x 16⅞ x 10⅛″ (12.5 x 42.8 x 25.7 cm). Designed in collaboration with D. J. De Vries, A. Macchi Cassia, G. Pasini, S. Pasqui. Manufactured by Ing. C. Olivetti & C., S.p.A.

Three study models for LOGOS 50/60 ELECTRONIC PRINTING CALCULATOR. Polystyrene.

DIVISUMMA 18 ELECTRONIC PRINTING CALCULATOR.
1972. Cast-injected ABS plastic body, flexible syn-
thetic rubber skin, melamine, 1⅞ x 9¾ x 5″ (4.8 x
24.8 x 12.7 cm). Designed in collaboration with
A. De Gregori, D. J. De Vries, A. Macchi Cassia,
G. Pasini, S. Pasqui, De Diana. Manufactured by
Ing. C. Olivetti & C., S.p.A. The Museum of Modern
Art, New York, gift of the manufacturer.

DIVISUMMA 28 ELECTRONIC PRINTING CALCULATOR.
1972. Cast-injected ABS plastic body, flexible synthetic rubber skin, melamine, 3⅜ x 8¼ x 9¹⁄₁₆″ (8.5
x 21 x 23 cm). Designed in collaboration with A. De
Gregori, D. J. De Vries, A. Macchi Cassia, G. Pasini,
S. Pasqui. Manufactured by Ing. C. Olivetti & C.,
S.p.A. The Museum of Modern Art, New York, gift
of the manufacturer.

A 4 PROGRAMMABLE ACCOUNTING-INVOICING MACHINE.
1973. Cast-injected ABS plastic body, aluminum,
11 x 20⅞ x 19¼″ (28 x 53 x 49 cm). Designed in collaboration with D. J. De Vries, A. Macchi Cassia, G.
Pasini, S. Pasqui. Manufactured by Ing. C. Olivetti &
C., S.p.A.

LEXIKON 82 ELECTRIC PORTABLE TYPEWRITER. 1972-73.
Cast-injected ABS plastic body, 4¾ x 14⅞ x 15⅜″
(12 x 37.8 x 39.1 cm). Designed in collaboration with
A. Macchi Cassia, G. Pasini, S. Pasqui. Manufac-
tured by Ing. C. Olivetti & C., S.p.A. The Museum of
Modern Art, New York, gift of the manufacturer.

"MONITOR 15" TELEVISION. 1975. Semi-expanded
polystyrene with scratch-proof and anti-reflection
paint, 10¼ x 13 x 11″ (26.1 x 33.2 x 27.9 cm).
Designed in collaboration with Dario Bellini. Manufactured by Brionvega, S.p.A.

Marco Zanuso, Richard Sapper. "BLACK 201" TELE-
VISION. 1969. Metacrylic resin body, 11⅝ x 12⅝ x
11¾″ (29.5 x 32 x 29.8 cm). Manufactured by
Brionvega, S.p.A. The Museum of Modern Art, New
York, gift of the manufacturer.

YAMAHA STEREO CASSETTE DECK, model TC 800 GL.
1974. ABS plastic body, 3⅞ x 12¼ x 12¼″ (9.8 x

31.2 x 31.2 cm). Designed in collaboration with
Dario Bellini. Manufactured by Nippon Gakki Co.,
Ltd., Japan. The Museum of Modern Art, New York,
gift of the manufacturer.

TES 401 TEXT-EDITING SYSTEM. 1978. Cast-injected
ABS plastic body and lid, 9½ x 23¾ x 20⅝″ (24 x
60.5 x 52.5 cm). Designed in collaboration with A.
Macchi Cassia, G. Pasini, S. Pasqui. Manufactured
by Ing. C. Olivetti & C., S.p.A.

LOGOS 80 ELECTRONIC PRINTING CALCULATOR. 1978.
Cast-injected ABS plastic body, 4⅜ x 12⅛ x 11¾″
(11 x 31 x 30 cm). Designed in collaboration with A.
Macchi Cassia, G. Pasini, S. Pasqui. Manufactured
by Ing. C. Olivetti & C., S.p.A. The Museum of Modern Art, New York, gift of the manufacturer.

LETTERA 10 PORTABLE TYPEWRITER. 1976-77. Cast-
injected ABS plastic body, 4¾ x 9⁷⁄₁₆ x 9⅜″ (12 x
24 x 23.8 cm). Designed in collaboration with
A. Macchi Cassia, G. Pasini, S. Pasqui. Manufactured by Ing. C. Olivetti & C., S.p.A.

ET 111 ELECTRONIC TYPEWRITER. 1983. Cast-injected
ABS plastic case, metacrylic resin, 6⅝ x 27¾ x
18³⁄₁₆″ (16.9 x 70.5 x 46.3 cm). Manufactured by
Ing. C. Olivetti & C., S.p.A.

"PORTATONE" PORTABLE ELECTRONIC ORGAN, model PS
6100. 1984. ABS plastic body and aluminum, 37¾
x 46⅞ x 10¾″ (96 x 119 x 27.3 cm). Designed in collaboration with Dario Bellini. Manufactured by Nippon
Gakki Co., Ltd., Japan.

"ROBOT" ROTATING ANTENNA. 1980. Black enameled
ABS plastic, 17¼ x 5⅞ x 11¾″ (44 x 15 x 30 cm).
Designed in collaboration with Dario Bellini. Manu-
factured by Brionvega, S.p.A. The Museum of
Modern Art, New York, gift of the designer.

"MINIDECA" THERMOS. 1983. Polypropylene and
painted stainless steel sheeting, 11 x 9¹⁄₁₆ x 7¹⁄₁₆″
(28 x 23 x 18 cm). Designed in collaboration with
Dario Bellini. Manufactured by Zojirushi Corporation, Japan.

"CLASS" WATER FAUCET. 1978. Chromed brass fusion, 6¼ x 6¾ x 3" (15.8 x 17 x 7.6 cm). Designed in collaboration with Dario Bellini. Manufactured by Ideal Standard, S.p.A.

"ECLIPSE" LOW-VOLTAGE SPOTLIGHT. 1985. Die-cast aluminum, polyamide-reinforced fiberglass. Designed in collaboration with Dario Bellini. Manufactured by Erco Leuchten GmbH, Germany.

"ECLIPSE" LOW-VOLTAGE SPOTLIGHT. 1985. Die-cast aluminum, polyamide-reinforced fiberglass. Designed in collaboration with Dario Bellini. Manufactured by Erco Leuchten GmbH, Germany.

"ECLIPSE" LOW-VOLTAGE SPOTLIGHT. 1985. Die-cast aluminum, polyamide-reinforced fiberglass. Designed in collaboration with Dario Bellini. Manufactured by Erco Leuchten GmbH, Germany.

ELECTRONIC TYPEWRITER, project. 1985. Cast-injected ABS plastic body, folded sheet metal, 7⅛ x 22⅞ x 20⅞" (18 x 58 x 53 cm). Manufactured by Ing. C. Olivetti & C., S.p.A.

ETP 55 PORTABLE ELECTRONIC TYPEWRITER. 1985-86. Cast-injected ABS plastic body, 4⅞ x 16⅛ x 13" (12.5 x 41 x 33 cm). Manufactured by Ing. C. Olivetti & C., S.p.A.

Claes Oldenburg. FLOOR CONE. 1962. Synthetic polymer paint on canvas, filled with foam rubber and cardboard boxes, 53¾" x 11'4" x 56" (136.5 x 345.4 x 142 cm). The Museum of Modern Art, New York, gift of Philip Johnson.

Piero Gatti, Cesare Paolini, Franco Teodoro. "SACCO" Bean Bag CHAIR. 1969. Polyurethane pellets and leather, 45½ x 19¾" (130 x 85 cm). Manufactured by Zanotta, S.p.A. The Museum of Modern Art, New York, gift of the manufacturer.

TABLE. 1960. Plywood veneer, 29⅛ x 35½ x 35½" (74 x 90 x 90 cm). Manufactured by Pedretti; Gavina; and Knoll. Awarded the 1962 Compasso d'Oro prize.

"932/2" ARMCHAIR, SINGLE-SEAT VERSION. 1965. Originally foam rubber; later, injected polyurethane foam and Dacron padding, leather upholstery, 24⅜ x 36⅝ x 33½" (62 x 93 x 85 cm). Manufactured by Cassina, S.p.A. The Museum of Modern Art, New York, gift of the manufacturer.

Le Corbusier (Charles-Edouard Jeanneret), Pierre Jeanneret, Charlotte Perriand. "FAUTEUIL GRAND CONFORT, PETIT MODÈLE," EASY CHAIR. 1928. Chrome-plated tubular steel, down-filled leather cushions, 25 x 29¾ x 27¾" (63.5 x 75.5 x 70.5 cm). Manufactured by Heidi Weber, Switzerland. The Museum of Modern Art, New York, gift of Phyllis B. Lambert.

"AMANTA" MODULAR LOUNGE CHAIR. 1966. Molded polyester reinforced with fiberglass, 28 x 31⅞ x 31⅞" (71 x 81 x 81 cm). Manufactured by B & B Italia, S.p.A.

"TENERIDE" OFFICE CHAIR, project. 1970. "Self-skinning" polyurethane, 33½ x 26¾ x 23⅝" (85 x 68 x 60 cm). Prototype developed at Centro Cassina, S.p.A.

"CHIARA" FLOOR LAMP. 1964. Stainless steel, 57½ x 27¹⁵⁄₁₆ x 20" (146 x 71 x 51 cm). Manufactured by Flos, S.p.A.

"AREA" HANGING LAMP. 1974. Non-woven polyester, porcelain. Shade, 19¹¹⁄₁₆ x 19¹¹⁄₁₆" (50 x 50cm). Designed in collaboration with Giorgio Origlia. Manufactured by Artemide, S.p.A.

"LE STELLE" ARMCHAIR. 1974. Tubular steel structure, polyurethane foam anchored to frame with nylon cord, Dacron-filled cushions, quilted fabric upholstery closed with zippers, 30⅞ x 51⅛ x 33⅞" (78.5 x 130 x 86 cm). Manufactured by B & B Italia, S.p.A.

"LE BAMBOLE" SIDE CHAIR. 1972. Differential density polyurethane, Dacron padding, fabric upholstery, 28⅜ x 31½ x 34¼" (72 x 80 x 87 cm). Manufactured by B & B Italia, S.p.A.

"LE BAMBOLE" ARMCHAIR. 1972. Differential density

polyurethane, Dacron padding, fabric upholstery, 28⅜ x 47¼ x 35½" (72 x 120 x 90 cm). Manufactured by B & B Italia, S.p.A. Awarded the 1979 Compasso d'Oro prize.

"LE BAMBOLE" SOFA. 1972. Differential density polyurethane, Dacron padding, fabric upholstery, 28⅜ x 66⅛ x 35½" (72 x 168 x 90 cm). Manufactured by B & B Italia, S.p.A.

"CAB" SIDE CHAIR. 1976. Enameled steel frame, leather upholstery closed with zippers, 32¼ x 20½ x 18½" (82 x 52 x 47 cm). Designed in collaboration with Centro Design e Comunicazione, Cassina. Manufactured by Cassina, S.p.A. The Museum of Modern Art, New York, gift of the manufacturer.

"CAB" ARMCHAIR. 1978. Enameled steel frame, leather upholstery closed with zippers, 32¼ x 23⅝ x 20½" (82 x 60 x 52 cm). Designed in collaboration with Centro Design e Comunicazione, Cassina. Manufactured by Cassina, S.p.A. The Museum of Modern Art, New York, gift of Atelier International Ltd.

"TENTAZIONI" DINING CHAIR. 1973. Steel frame on wooden base. ABS plastic, polyurethane foam and polyester padding, leather upholstery, 32¹¹⁄₁₆ x 30⁵⁄₁₆ x 24⅜" (83 x 77 x 62 cm). Manufactured by Cassina, S.p.A.

"BREAK" DINING CHAIR. 1976. Steel frame, "self-skinning" polyurethane foam, and leather or fabric upholstery with leather piping, closed with zippers, 33½ x 22 x 20¹⁄₁₆" (85 x 56 x 51 cm). Manufactured by Cassina, S.p.A.

"IL COLONNATO" TABLE. 1977. Marble, 28¾ x 55⅛ x 55⅛" (73 x 140 x 140 cm). Manufactured by Cassina, S.p.A.

VITRINE. 1983-84. Stainless steel enameled with Nextel paint, 82½ x 39⅜ x 39⅜" (210 x 100 x 100 cm). Designed in collaboration with Dario Bellini, Giovanna Bonfanti. Manufactured by Ing. C.

Olivetti & C., S.p.A. Made for "The Treasury of San Marco" exhibition, 1984-87.

"PERSONA" OFFICE CHAIR. 1979-84. Aluminum and steel structure; polyamide-reinforced fiberglass cover; fabric upholstery, 36¼ x 27⁹⁄₁₆ x 27⁹⁄₁₆" (92 x 70 x 70 cm). Designed in collaboration with Dieter Thiel. Manufactured by Vitra International AG, Germany.

"FIGURA" OFFICE CHAIR. 1979-84. Aluminum and steel structure, plywood, Trevira CS padding, leather or fabric upholstery, 35⁷⁄₁₆ x 27⁹⁄₁₆ x 27⁹⁄₁₆" (90 x 70 x 70 cm). Designed in collaboration with Dieter Thiel. Manufactured by Vitra International AG, Germany.

"FORTE ROSSO" BENCH. 1985. Red Indian Sandstone, 22¹⁄₁₆ x 89¾ x 39⅜" (56 x 228 x 100 cm). Made for "The Golden Eye" exhibition at the Cooper-Hewitt Museum, New York, 1985.

Danilo Allegri: 55

Aldo Ballo: 16 (bottom), 22, 24 (right), 25 (left), 26 (lower left, lower right), 27 (top, bottom), 36 (upper right), 50 (lower left), 51, 53 (bottom), 56 (left, right), 57, 58 (left, right), 59, 60 (left, upper right, lower right), 62, 63 (left, right), 64

George Barrow: 50 (top)

Bella e Ruggeri: 44 (top, bottom)

Mario Carrieri: 46, 47 (top, bottom), 65

Giorgio Casali: 52, 53 (top)

Colore Industriale: 12 (bottom), 13 (top, bottom), 14, 15 (top), 16 (top), 17, 19 (top, lower right), 23 (left, right), 24 (left), 25 (right), 31

Erco Leuchten: 45 (top, bottom)

Bruno Falchi and Liderno Salvador: 54

Ezio Frea: 11 (right), 26 (top), 28 (top, bottom), 30, 32 (top, left, center, right), 33, 34, 35, 38 (top, bottom), 39, 40, 41

Seth Joel: 36 (lower right), 48 (bottom)

Kate Keller: 11 (left), 29 (upper right, lower right)

Mark Lauriller for Ranzini: 37 (top)

Robert McElroy: 48 (top)

Antonia Mulas: 20

Maria Mulas: Frontispiece

The Museum of Modern Art: 16 (bottom), 50 (lower right)

Mali Olatunji: 18, 21, 29 (left), 61

Olivetti Studio Design: 12 (top), 15 (bottom)

Photo Team: 36 (upper left, lower left)

Pollitzer, Strong & Meyer: 37 (bottom), 43

Stan Reis: 19 (lower left)

Manfred Rieker Studio: 66, 67, 68, 69

Soichi Sunami: 10

Nippon Gakki: 42

Zojirushi: 44 (left)